▶ △ ◀ ◁ ▼ ◁ ▶ △ ◀

BIRTH DAY

▲ △ ◄ ◁ ▼ ◁ ► △ ◀

BIRTH DAY

A CELEBRATION OF BABY ANIMALS

by
MIDAS DEKKERS

Scientific
BOOKS FOR YOUNG READERS
American

W. H. Freeman and Company
New York

List of Illustrations

Othmar Baumli: pp. 4-5, 18, 30, 31, 44-45, 64; *Theres Buholzer:* pp. 34, 54, 55; *Andreas Fischer-Nagel:* pp. 2, 10-13, 16, 19, 20, 24, 25, 33, 36, 38, 39, 48-49, 56-63, 67, 68, 75, 80, 82, 84-86; *Elvig Hansen:* pp. 14, 15, 22, 23, 28, 32, 35, 41, 52, 53, 79; *Jacana:* p. 87 (Albert Visage); *Felix Labhardt:* pp. 8 (also cover page), 74; *Neil McLeod:* pp. 72, 77; *Angela Meder:* pp. 26, 27; *Max Meier:* pp. 69, 76; *Dorothy Morris:* p. 40; *Hans Reinhard:* frontispiece; *Manfred Rogl:* pp. 17, 29, 70, 71, 78; *Wolfgang Sauer:* pp. 42, 43, 81; *Jin Xuqi:* pp 50, 66.

Illustrations selected by Midas Dekkers
Text adapted by Justine Korman
Text Design by Marsha Cohen/Parallelogram Graphics
Cover Design by Debora S. Smith

Originally published in Dutch under the title
Het grote moment: Hoe dieren geboren worden

© 1989 Kinderbuchverlag Luzern AG

Dekkers, Midas, 1946-
    Birth day : a celebration of baby animals / Midas Dekkers
        p.   cm.
    ISBN 0-7167-6581-0 (hardcover)
    1. Parturition—Juvenile literature. 2. Animals—Infancy—Juvenile literature. [1. Birth. 2. Animals—Infancy.]
    I. Title
    QP285.D45   1995
    599'.039—dc20
    94-35394

        CIP   AC

Printed in Mexico

▶ △ ◀ △ ▼ △ ▶ △ ◀

CONTENTS

Title Page
All kittens are born with blue eyes, but the color may change during their first few months of life.

◀ *This mother duck takes good care of her five fuzzy ducklings.*

▲ △ ◄ ◁ **I** ▷ ▶ △ ◀

A NEW LIFE

Where does new life come from? For a long time, people did not know for sure. They watched flies crawl out of rotten meat. They spotted mice on loaves of stale bread. And they saw lice creep out of dust and dirt. So they thought that the meat, the bread, and the dirt gave birth to the flies, the mice, and the lice!

Over the years, as people looked more closely, they discovered that baby flies hatch out of eggs other flies lay in spoiled meat. Mice come to eat bread that is left out. And lice hatch from louse eggs laid in the dirt.

Flies, mice, and lice all have mothers and fathers—just like you!

Every species—kind of creature—on earth can create more of its own kind. This is called reproduction. Reproduction is an important part of life because in time, every living thing dies—sometimes from an injury that cannot heal or an illness that cannot get better. For a species to survive, young animals must be born to replace the ones that die.

But how are baby animals born? Perhaps you have a cat that has had kittens. You saw her belly get bigger and bigger.

Or maybe you remember when your little brother or sister was about to be born. You saw your mother's belly get bigger and bigger! Cats, humans, and many other animal babies grow inside the womb, a special place in the mother's belly, until they are ready to come out. This period of time is called pregnancy.

Other animals, like birds and some fish and reptiles, develop in eggs outside their mothers until they are strong enough to break out.

The beginning of a new life is a beautiful event, but not everyone is lucky enough to see the big moment happening.

Sometimes the great moment takes place late at night while people are asleep. Sometimes the mother animal won't let anyone watch the birth of her babies because she's afraid someone might hurt them. And of course, most births take place in the wild, with no people around at all. Even if you never get to watch an actual birth, the pictures in this book will give you a chance to see for yourself what happens before, during, and after the big moment.

▲△◄◁2▷►△◄
BEGINNINGS AND BELLY BUTTONS

Every animal starts life the same way—as two tiny cells. Cells are the microscopic building blocks of life. There are many different kinds of cells, like blood cells, skin cells, and brain cells. A full-grown animal is made of millions and millions of cells, but they start when an egg cell from the mother meets a sperm cell from the father.

In many animals, including humans, the egg and the sperm meet inside a place in the mother's body called the womb. For this to happen, the animals must mate. Many male animals have a body part like a squirt gun, called a penis. The male slips his penis into an opening in the female's body called a vagina. The vagina is also the opening where the baby comes out.

The tiny egg is very hard for the even tinier sperm to find. So the male sends millions of sperm cells into the female each time they mate.

Sperm cells have long tails, which they whip back and forth to swim. Each sperm cell swims toward the egg. Sometimes none of them find it. But usually, sperm and egg do meet, and

◄ *The fox pup snuggles happily in its mother's warm fur.*

▼ *The stub on this kitten's belly is all that's left of its umbilical cord. The cord brought food and air to the kitten while it was inside the mother cat's womb. Soon the stub will dry up and fall off—leaving only a belly button!*

fertilization occurs. Together, the sperm and egg form a single cell, a mixture of the mother and father, that will grow and divide into more and more cells to become an embryo—the beginning of a baby!

What is it like being born? No one knows! You don't remember your own birth. But you do have a souvenir of your birth in the middle of your belly—your belly button, or navel. It marks the spot where you were separated from your mother's body. Your belly button serves no purpose after you are born—except to be ticklish!

When you first became an embryo in your mother's womb, you were linked to her by a slender, fleshy tube called the umbilical cord. Since you were too little to eat or even breathe for yourself, food and oxygen passed from your mother's body down the umbilical cord to you.

▶ *Birds don't have belly buttons because they have babies in a different way.*

Right after birth, or delivery, your umbilical cord was tied off and cut. A little stump was left, which dried up and fell off, leaving your belly button!

Dogs and cats have belly buttons, too. They're just not easy to see under all that fur. Most of the time, a mother cat or dog bites off the umbilical cord after birth.

Animal and human babies have to get big and strong before they can live without their umbilical cords or the

◀ *The great moment! A kitten comes into the world.*

▼ *The mother cat licks her baby dry.*

13

▲ *This guinea pig is only a half hour old and already exploring its surroundings!*

◄ *Many animals are born bald, blind, and helpless. But guinea pigs come into the world furry and ready for action!*

safety of their mothers' bodies. They do more growing before birth than they ever will again! Just before birth, you were already 2,500 times as big and a *billion* times as heavy as you were at conception.

A whale, which also starts out as small as a pinpoint, often weighs as much as 5,500 pounds at birth. Then it gains another 200 pounds every day!

▲ *This is a stork's egg. When the baby is ready to hatch, it pecks a little hole in the shell with its egg tooth.*
Then it pecks a bigger hole.
As the little bird stretches, the hole gets bigger.
Finally, the baby stork hatches!

▼ *These baby barn owls have recently hatched, and their mother is sheltering them under her wings. When they were still in their eggs, blood vessels in the yolk brought food to them. Each growing bird absorbed the yolk and then the blood vessels. When the food was all gone, the birds hatched!*

▼ *The mother duck pads her nest with soft*
feathers to keep her eggs cozy.

▼ *In bad weather, stork parents keep their babies warm and dry under their wings.*

▶ △ ◁ △ **3** △ ▶ △ ◀
MILK AND EGGS

Even once an animal is big and strong enough to enter the world and lose its umbilical cord or shell, it still needs to have a source of food nearby.

Many baby animals, including people, drink milk right from their mothers' breasts. This is called nursing.

A cow makes milk to feed her calf. A jenny, or female donkey, gives milk to her foal. Dogs and cats feed milk to their puppies and kittens. This milk has everything the newborn calf, donkey, kitten, or puppy needs for the first part of its life.

◀ *When this female donkey's baby is born, she will feed it with her milk.*

Animals that nurse their young with milk are called mammals. Mammals have skin with fur or hair. Cats, dogs, and people are all mammals. So are whales, even though they have very little hair.

How do mammal mothers make milk? Special milk glands take food from the mother's blood and turn it into milk. Then the milk travels through the breasts to the nipples, which are sometimes called teats.

Baby mammals must find milk as soon as they are born. Sometimes they need help. Kittens are born blind and without much of a sense of smell. So the mother cat presses her kittens'

▼ *After a meal of milk, these kids rest. Maybe their mother should be resting too!*

noses to her teats. The kitten pushes its paws against the teats. This "milking tread" starts the milk flowing. Sometimes when grown-up cats are feeling playful, they tread on your tummy—but they won't get any milk!

◄ *Goat kids butt their mother's udder to start her milk flow. Kids nurse for two or three months. They can give their mother a rough time with all that butting!*

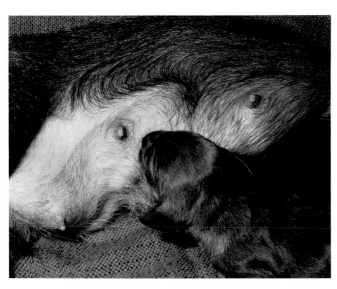

Right after birth, dachshund puppies look for the milk fountain, the teats, and start nursing.

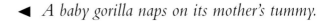

Young mammals drink from their mothers until they're big enough to eat by themselves. Even then, babies still want milk. A baby gorilla can eat leaves when it's only two and a half months old. But it will still nurse for over a year!

Nursing usually ends when the baby gorilla starts to bite. This hurts the mother gorilla. Besides, she may not have any more milk, or she may have a new baby to feed.

Most baby animals like nursing. It makes them feel happy and cozy and close to their mother. They don't want to stop. The mother pushes them away to make them understand they are too grown up to nurse. Teaching the baby animal not to nurse anymore is called weaning.

Once they are weaned, most animals never drink milk again. Many people, of course, enjoy drinking cow's milk. And sometimes cats do too. But that's not the same as nursing.

◀ *The mother gorilla holds her nursing baby tenderly in her arm, just like a human mother.*

You can't buy cat's milk or human milk in a store. We are so used to this that when we say milk, we mean cow's milk. We call human milk "mother's milk." But of course cow's milk or cat's milk is also mother's milk—if you're a calf or a kitten!

▼ *Although birds don't nurse their young, they take good care of their babies even before hatching. This female parakeet turns her eggs often to warm them evenly.*

There are big differences between the milks of different mammals. Whale's milk contains three times as much fat as the milk of people or cows, because a young whale needs a thick layer of fat to keep it warm in the ocean. And rabbit's milk has more protein than human milk. That's why rabbits grow so fast. Humans like the taste of cow's milk because it tastes a little like our own.

▼ *Barn owls also turn their eggs.*

A mammal baby stays inside its mother's womb until it has lungs for breathing, a skin for protection against germs, and of course, a mouth for drinking milk.

Some animal babies don't wait to grow much inside their mothers. Baby birds leave their mother's body before body, picking up a yolk, a white, and finally, a shell.

The shell protects the unborn chick and keeps it from drying out. But it can't protect the chick against cold. So mother birds—and sometimes fathers—sit on their eggs to keep them warm.

1

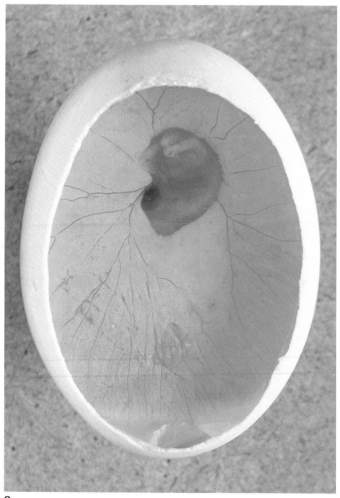

2

they have lungs, skin, or a beak. The chick is still as small as a pinhead. The tiny embryo passes through its mother's

Keeping the eggs warm while the embryo grows is called incubation.

Inside the shell, the bird embryo floats

on top of the yolk. Heat from the parent's body helps the embryo grow and develop blood vessels. These blood vessels take food from the yolk.

Baby birds grow quickly. The photos show an unborn duck growing inside its egg. After six days (1), an eye is visible as (3), you can see a duck's bill. After another week (4), the egg tooth can be seen on the tip of the bill. At the end of the fourth week, when all the yolk and white have been absorbed by the duckling, it is time to hatch! The baby duck uses the egg tooth to crack open its shell.

3

4

a dark spot. After ten days (2), an ear appears as a small spot behind the eye. Two weeks after the egg has been laid

Most baby birds aren't able to feed themselves right after hatching. So their mothers or fathers bring them worms, caterpillars, seeds, and other foods to eat, stuffing the food into the baby bird's beak. Sometimes the parents chew the food for their babies too.

Even though birds don't nurse their young, some birds do make a sort of milk for their babies. Pigeons and parakeets make milky fluid in the crop, a part of the stomach. Then they bring up the milk and feed it to their babies!

Birds aren't the only babies to hatch from eggs. Insects also lay eggs to repro-

▼ *This parakeet mom feeds her biggest chick with food from her crop.*

duce. There are more insects in the world than any other kind of animal.

Insect eggs are so small that most people don't notice how beautiful they can be. Ladybugs lay bright-yellow eggs, which later turn green. The mother glues the eggs to a leaf and then just flies away.

But the babies will have plenty of food when they hatch because mother ladybugs often glue their eggs to plants covered with tiny bugs called aphids. These aphids make a tasty meal for baby ladybugs.

▼ *A ladybug lays shiny yellow eggs and glues them to a leaf.*

Snails lay dozens of clear eggs in small holes in the ground. You can see the babies growing inside them. Baby snails hatch when their shells are finished growing.

Toads lay their eggs in water because the shells are too thin to keep the eggs from drying out. Hundreds of eggs come out of the mother's body in two long strings. Then the father fertilizes the eggs by adding his sperm.

▼ *Snails lay their eggs in a hole in the ground.*

▼ *After about two weeks, young snails hatch from their eggs, complete with their shell "home."*

In a human female, an egg ripens every month. If the egg is fertilized by a male's sperm, a baby will grow inside a sac like the white of a chicken's egg. This is called the amniotic sac. Like a chicken's egg, the sac keeps the embryo safe until it is ready to be born.

If the egg is not fertilized it leaves the body. The almost invisible little egg goes out through the vagina, the same opening babies use to be born. In a way, your mother lays eggs!

▼ *Toads lay strings of eggs around water plants.*

35

▶ △ ◀ △ 4 ▷ ▶ △ ◀
BIRTH DAY

Being born usually doesn't take very long, but an animal's whole life depends on this big moment. An animal must be born at just the right time. If it is born too early, the baby may not be able to survive outside its mother's body. If it is born too late, it may be too big to slide out through the narrow opening.

Baby animals don't have clocks or calendars. The time of birth depends on their growth. When the baby is ready to be born, its body sends a signal to the mother by way of a special chemical, or hormone. This hormone travels in the mother's bloodstream. Like a switch inside a computer, the birth hormone tells the mother's body to change from "Keep baby inside" to "Let baby out."

The length of time a baby spends growing in its mother's womb is different for each kind of mammal. This time is called gestation. Large mammals take longer to gestate than small ones.

◀ *When hamster babies are born, they are only about one inch long, hairless, and blind.*

A young mouse is ready to be born after only twenty days. An elephant takes twenty months—almost two years! Medium-sized mammals have a medium gestation period: nine weeks for a dog or cat; five months for a sheep; and eleven months for a horse. Human babies usually grow in their mother's womb for nine months.

Animal mothers sense when it's time

▼ *To give birth, the female hamster stands on her hind legs and bends her head down.*

to give birth. They prepare a nest or find another safe place. House cats crawl under beds or into closets. Rabbits dig holes and shed fur that they use to make the hole soft and warm.

A baby mammal can't come out of its mother's belly on its own. They are out. As the time of birth nears, the womb muscles contract—push and squeeze—more and more often. These contractions are called labor.

Most animal mothers lie down to birth their babies, but giraffes give birth standing up. The baby giraffe

▲ *The mother hamster starts to free her baby from the amniotic sac even while it is still sliding out of her body.*

▲ *Once the baby is born, the mother hamster bites off the umbilical cord.*

much too weak for that. So Mom does the work! She uses the muscles of her stomach and womb to push the baby drops six and a half feet to the ground, turning in midair so it won't land on its head!

Animal babies are born at certain times of the year—and for good reason. A fawn or lamb born in winter would not survive the cold. And its mother would not be able to find enough food to make milk for her baby.

For babies to be born when the sun is warm and there is plenty of food, parents must mate at the right time. This period is called the mating season.

Because her pregnancy lasts five months, a ewe—female sheep—must mate in the fall for her lambs to be born in the spring. How does she

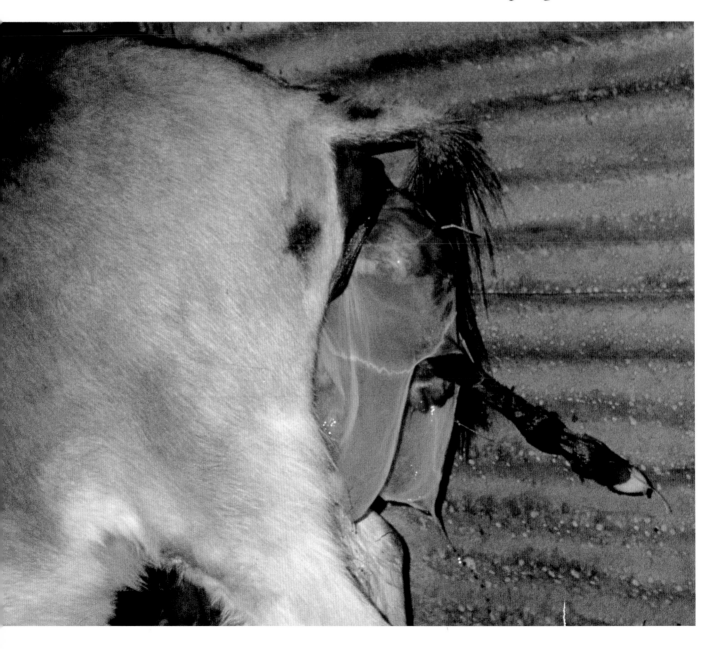

know the right time has arrived? She waits for the days to start getting shorter. The ewe will let the ram mate with her only when autumn arrives. Birds mate in the spring, so they wait for the days to grow longer. Some animals, such as mice and rats, can mate year-round, but they usually take a rest in winter. Most mammal babies are born head first, so they can breathe as soon as possible. If the baby is born rear first, it may suffocate when it tries to breathe while its head is still inside the womb.

▲ *A mother guinea pig eats her baby's amniotic sac.*
◄ *This donkey foal comes out with its front legs and head first. The amniotic sac breaks, allowing the donkey to breathe.*
► *The mother goat cleans her newborn kid with her tongue.*

Even though most baby animals can't push themselves out of their mothers' bodies, many help with their own births without even thinking about it. For example, legs can get in the way during birth. A calf keeps them extended on either side of its head. Little "socks" of soft tissue cushion the calf's hooves so that the amniotic sac and birth opening are not injured. The little socks disappear later.

Right after birth, the mother deer stands up, and the umbilical cord tears. Then she eats the amniotic sac.

A baby camel's hump folds down on its back so it can fit through the birth opening. And luckily, a porcupine's quills are still soft when it's born.

Bats like to do everything backward. They sleep hanging upside down. To give birth, the mother bat raises her head and the baby comes out feet first.

Whales and dolphins are born tail first. While giving birth, a whale mom looks like she has two tails—her own big one and the baby's little one below it.

When a baby mammal is born, it is still wrapped in the amniotic sac. Often the sac bursts during birth. If it does not, the mother may bite it open and lick it off or eat it.

When the amniotic sac bursts, some liquid spills out. The baby has been living in this amniotic fluid, like a fish in a bowl. The liquid is not for swimming, though. It protects the baby from bumps and shocks. An unborn puppy needs about a cup full of amniotic fluid. A kitten needs only about two

▼ *This little fawn is only a half hour old. It is already trying to stand.*

Mammal mothers do the work at birth, but baby birds must get out of the egg by themselves. After all that hard work, a duckling lies wet and tired in its nest.

tablespoons. When a baby calf is born, a whole bucketful of amniotic fluid comes gushing out!

After the baby is born and the umbilical cord is broken, the mother pulls the other end of the cord out of her body. This end is attached to an organ called the placenta. While the baby is in the womb, the placenta takes food and oxygen from the mother's blood and passes it down the umbilical cord.

Now that they are no longer needed, the mother eats the placenta and umbilical cord—the afterbirth. It doesn't look very tasty, but it is full of nutrients to help her regain her strength. Eating the afterbirth also helps keep away predators, who would otherwise smell that a baby had been born.

Only seals and hippopotamuses won't eat their afterbirth. They leave it for hungry seagulls or crocodiles.

The slippery amniotic sac also helps the baby come out more easily. But even so, live birth is still hard! Egg laying is much easier. Just look in the kitchen and see how smooth an egg is. And when the hen lays it, the shell is not as hard as it is later. So it comes out even more easily. Snail, frog, and fish eggs also are very soft. They simply slide out.

An egg makes birth much easier for

the mother. But it makes things much harder for the baby! While a bird embryo is growing, the eggshell is per-fect for protection. But when it's time to hatch, the shell becomes a prison. Imagine if you had to be born out of a chest or box that was nailed shut and that you had to get out all by yourself. A chick has that same problem when it's time to hatch.

When the big moment arrives, the

◄ *The mare licks her newborn foal dry with her big tongue. She warms her baby with her breath.*

▼ *The colt soon stands on its own wobbly legs.*

chick pecks a little hole in the flatter end of the egg with its egg tooth, letting in fresh air. The chick takes a big breath and turns a little in the egg. It pecks a second hole near the first, then a third, then a fourth, and so on. When it has made several holes, it can push away a piece of the shell.

Different birds break out of their shells in different ways. An owl hatchling makes a very neat circle of holes. But a baby chicken makes a much sloppier exit, pecking holes everywhere to get out of the egg as fast as possible.

At last, the chick is free! The mother bird dries her tired baby under her wings. An hour later, with its downy feathers fluffed up, the chick looks much bigger. How did it ever fit in that tiny egg?

The moment of birth is the biggest change in the life of any animal. Not only does the baby have to breathe by itself, it also has to eat its own food and survive in a whole new environment. That's a lot to do!

◄ *While the donkey grazes, her foal explores its world. Even though it's not quite a year old, the foal is almost as big as its mother.*

▶△◀◁ 5 ▷▶△◀
BOY OR GIRL?

When you were born, everyone knew right away whether you were a boy or a girl. But it's not so easy to tell with some animals. Male and female kittens look exactly the same for the first few weeks. Male and female pandas—even adults—look very much alike. Once some zookeepers put two male pandas together by mistake. Then they wondered why the couple didn't have any babies!

Why does one baby turn out to be a boy and another a girl? People used to think this depended on the mother. They had many ideas that seem funny to us now. For instance, they thought that if the mother slept on her left side,

her baby would be a boy. Or if she ate lots of sweets, it would be a girl.

Now we know that the father supplies two different kinds of sperm. One kind makes boys. The other kind makes girls. So the sperm that reaches the egg first "decides" what the baby will be. A human father makes about the same amount of each kind of sperm. So about as many boys as girls are born.

Some animal babies aren't born male or female! They become male or female only as they grow up. The babies inside certain reptile eggs turn male or female depending on how hot or cold their nest is.

When a toad's egg hatches, the baby that comes out, called a tadpole, doesn't look like a toad at all. It looks like a fish, with a long tail, and it must live in

◀ *The little panda cuddling its mother is a boy. But it looks just like a girl panda.*

51

water. After a few weeks, the tadpole starts to grow feet, and its tail starts to turn into a body. Gradually, the tadpole looks more and more like a toad. Then you can tell males and females apart, but it's still hard, even for other toads.

During the mating season, a male toad will eagerly jump onto any other toad. If the other toad croaks an angry protest, the male knows he's landed on another male by mistake.

◄ *A newborn toad is called a tadpole.*
▼ *Within two to three months, tadpoles become very small toads.*

Snails are even stranger. They are both male and female. Every snail produces both eggs and sperm. If no other snails are around, a snail can even mate with itself!

Before mating, snails "smooch" for hours. They press against each other and push each other up. They wave their heads back and forth, and keep from falling over by pushing calcium spikes, called love darts, into each other's feet. (The bottom of a snail's body is called its foot.) Then, the white sex opening appears on the right side of the snail's head! In most animals, the reproductive organs are found at the rear or bottom of the body. But snails are unusual!

Each snail injects sperm into the sex opening of its partner. When the eggs have been fertilized, the snail lays them in the ground. In early summer, baby snails will hatch from these eggs.

◄ *Each snail is both male and female. Before mating, snails cuddle with each other for a long time.*

▲ *Then they shoot off a love dart like this one. Finally, the snails inject sperm into each other.*

Maybe you've seen ants around an anthill carrying what look like grains of rice. The ants are really carrying around their babies!

When a tiny ant egg hatches, a worm-like creature called a larva comes out. The larva then spins itself a protective casing called a cocoon, which the parent carries on its back.

Inside the cocoon, the larva changes into a pupa. The pupa grows feelers, called antennas, and three pairs of legs, and its white skin becomes a sturdy shell.

Most insects are born this way. Since three-quarters of all the animals on earth are insects, this type of four-stage life—egg, larva, pupa, adult—is the most common.

Here is one way to see how a pupa develops. On a hot day, ask an adult for a small amount of chopped meat and put it outside. Flies love to eat chopped meat and to lay their eggs in it. With a little luck, you will see a female fly lay her eggs. Female flies usually lay more than a hundred eggs at a time!

◀ *The white grains among the ants in this picture are ant pupas.*

▶ *A common housefly lays her eggs.*

57

The next day you will find little white worms which have hatched from the eggs. These are fly larvas, called maggots. The maggots eat the meat and grow quickly.

After only one day, the maggots are twice as big! Their skin is too tight. So they shed their skin and grow a new one. The fly larvas keep eating and growing. They shed their skin three times. Then they pupate, or change into a pupa.

The maggots hatch from fly eggs. After about a day, the maggots shed their skin for the first time. This maggot will pupate soon. The pupa's soft, white skin becomes hard and reddish-brown.

Each maggot's outer skin gets darker and becomes a hard shell. The pupa lies still inside the shell, slowly changing into a fly.

In a few days, the young fly inflates a bubble on the top of its head. When the bubble gets big enough, it bursts the pupa shell!

Once the young fly hatches, you may be able to tell if it's male or female. Male flies have bigger eyes.

The common housefly hatches headfirst from the hard skin of its pupa. A fly is born! But it cannot fly until its wings are dry.

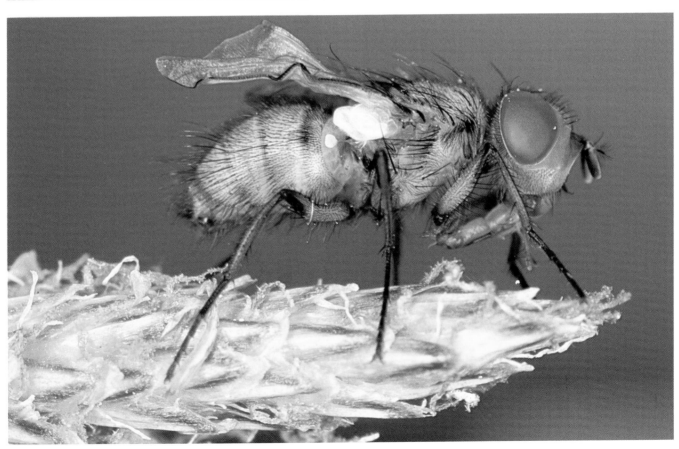

A butterfly also grows in four stages: egg, larva, pupa, and adult. A butterfly usually lays its eggs on the underside of a leaf. Moisture holds the eggs to the leaf and keeps them from drying out. After a few days, the butterfly larva chews itself

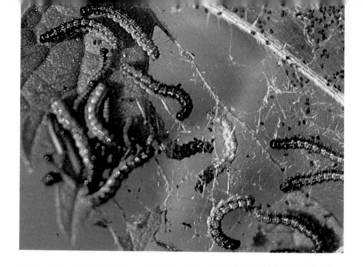

After about eight days, the butterfly eggs hatch. The new hatchlings are black-headed caterpillars. The caterpillars eat lots of leaves. The caterpillars grow and shed their skins. This picture shows the caterpillar after it has shed its old skin.

free. You've probably seen butterfly larvas—we call them caterpillars.

A caterpillar has two jaws on its head. It uses these jaws to chew up leaves. Caterpillars eat so fast they soon run out of leaves. So they send out threads, like spider's silk. Then they travel on these threads to other branches or trees, in search of more leaves.

The hungry caterpillar grows fast and soon sheds its skin. Often, the new skin has beautiful hairs, or spots of color.

After a few weeks, the caterpillar is ready to pupate. It attaches its rear section to a twig. Its skin becomes wrinkled and then splits behind the caterpillar's head. It sheds its skin, as it has many times before. Only this time

After five weeks, the caterpillar pupates. The pupa hangs motionless on a twig. Then the pupa's skin bursts. The green chrysalis emerges.

it emerges from the old skin not just a bigger caterpillar, but a pupa!

The pupa is covered by a pretty, shell-like skin, the chrysalis. At first the chrysalis is very light and soft. In time, the shell becomes darker and firmer and shrinks a little. Inside the chrysalis, the pupa is slowly becoming a butterfly.

The young butterfly's wings are folded up inside the chrysalis. By the end of two weeks, the chrysalis bursts, opening along its seams like a zipper.

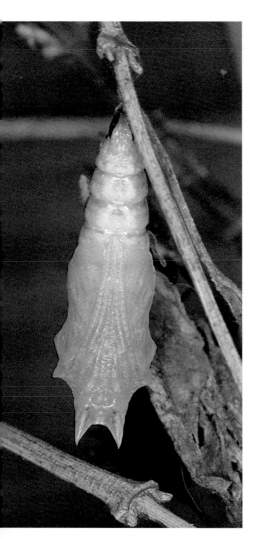
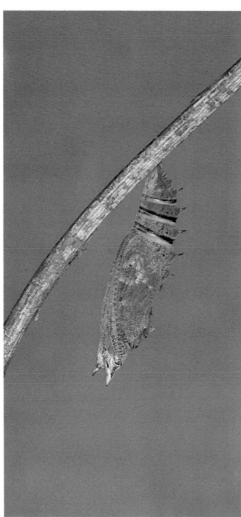
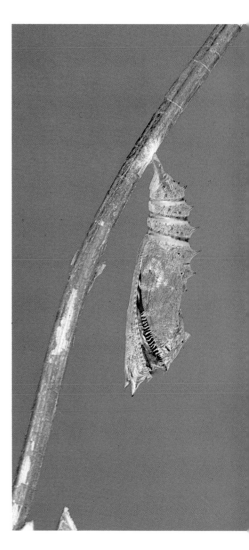

The pupa spends two weeks inside its chrysalis shell. In this picture, the butterfly is visible through the shell. The chrysalis splits open.

Head first, the butterfly works its way out of the shell. It unfolds its wet, wrinkled wings by pumping blood into them.

Why do insects go to all the trouble of growing in four separate stages?

Why doesn't a tiny butterfly or ant simply come out of the egg?

Adult insects have a hard shell. This rigid armor cannot expand, so insects must do all their growing while their skin is still soft.

The peacock butterfly works its way out of its shell head first. The butterfly unfolds its wings to dry.

6

ONE, TWO, A THOUSAND

Ducks can lay a dozen eggs at a time. But most of them do not become ducks. Many won't hatch at all. Some eggs and ducklings are eaten by other animals. Some simply are not strong enough to survive. But if every duck raised even five ducklings to adulthood, and those five ducklings had five more, the duck pond would be more feathers than water in no time! On the other hand, if ducks didn't hatch enough ducklings, there would soon be no ducks. Luckily, the number is usually just right.

Some human parents have a dozen children of different ages. But no human being has a dozen babies at once. Perhaps you know a set of twins, two babies born at the same time. Maybe you've even heard of triplets—that's three. Every once in a while, a mother might have four or five babies at once. That's a lot of diapers!

But for some animals, five babies isn't very many at all. A rabbit may have a litter of eight (octuplets). Pigs usually have ten or twelve piglets at a time. One female pig even had thirty! Birds often lay many eggs at a time. The blue tit holds the bird record—twenty-four eggs!

You can't know just by looking at a bird how many eggs it will lay. But you can tell from counting a mammal's teats how many children the mother can feed. Human mothers have two nipples, since they don't often have more than

◄ *This is a cluster—a family of ducks. The male duck swims a short distance from the mother and her ducklings to watch over the cluster.*

two babies at a time. Dogs and cats have six teats, and sows have even more.

Dogs are meant to have several puppies at a time. You might think it would be easier for a mother dog to have just one puppy. But often a single puppy is much bigger than a puppy from a mul-

The mother donkey doesn't let her woolly young foal out of her sight.

tiple litter. Several small babies come out of the mother's womb more easily than one big one. Animals with fewer offspring have a much harder job at birth.

Also, when a mother has only one baby at a time, she appears more concerned about losing it. A horse or cow keeps her foal or calf near her all day long. The mother monkey carries her baby with her for many months. Often the babies in a large litter aren't very well cared for—the parents don't seem to become upset if some of them die. But as with people, a single baby in the animal kingdom is usually well protected.

At birth, a baby panda is as small as a rat. It squeaks like a rat too! The mother panda is a thousand times bigger than her baby. She has to take very

◄ *Pandas usually have only one baby. Sometimes they have two, but the second one rarely survives. This panda holds her tiny baby tightly in her arms. The panda baby weighs only about three and a half ounces!*

good care of her tiny baby before it can manage on its own. If the baby panda dies, the mother has to wait a whole year before having another baby.

Some other mammals who usually have only one baby at a time are the elephant, the rhinoceros, the seal, and the bat. Some birds also have only one baby at a time. These birds usually live in

▼ *A female hamster is pregnant for only sixteen days. Then she brings six to twelve tiny hamsters into the world.*

places where they have few natural enemies. Emperor penguins, who live near
the South Pole, lay only one egg each
year. But rabbits, hamsters, and other
small rodents are on the menu for
many predators, so they have lots of
babies to replace those that are eaten.

In many animal mothers, the teats
give different amounts of milk. The
babies fight for the best milk fountain.

▼ *This wolf spider mother carries over a hundred
baby spiders on her back.*

▲ *The father barn owl works hard to bring mice home to his babies.*

The runt, or smallest member of a litter, is usually the baby who only gets the driest teat. If the runt doesn't get enough milk to grow strong, it can die.

The blue tit may be the bird that lays the most eggs, but there are other animals that lay far more. Toads and spiders lay hundreds of eggs at once, so even if many of them are eaten, there will still be plenty left.

But the all-time egg-laying record goes to the giant ocean sunfish, which lays thirty million eggs at a time!

Finding food for a lot of babies is hard work, so some animals adjust how many babies they have. For example, if food is scarce, an owl will lay fewer eggs. But when there are plenty of mice to go around, the barn owl lays many more eggs.

Most birds lay one egg a day. But owls take two days to lay an egg. And sometimes a mouse shortage doesn't happen until the owl has already begun to lay eggs. Owls have a solution for this: Instead of waiting for all her eggs to be laid, the mother starts warming the first egg. This means her eggs will hatch at different times.

The youngest owlet is the weakest and smallest. But the oldest baby, which

screams the loudest, gets the most food. When the oldest is done, the younger birds may get some food. This ensures that at least some of the babies will survive. If the food were shared equally, there would be so little that all the owlets would die.

▲ *Baby owls screech for food!*
▼ *Sometimes the father gives the mouse to an owlet who is already full. The owlet passes the furry meal to its hungry brother or sister.*

7

A HOME FOR THE BABIES

Mammals start life in the nicest nest of all—inside their mother's womb. There they are safe and warm. Some fish and lizards keep their young in their bellies for a while too. But birds can't. If they had babies in their wombs, they would be too heavy to fly! That's why birds lay eggs and build soft nests.

Many birds build nests with anything they can find. They use straw, hay, sand and saliva, feathers, even plastic bags and spiderwebs. In the cozy nest, the eggs are warmed by the outside of the mother's belly instead of the inside. Mother birds have a bald patch on their tummies that helps them heat their eggs.

Birds hide their nests to keep their babies safe from predators. Many nests are the same color as their surroundings. This is called camouflage.

Storks don't need camouflage. They build nests in high places that most other animals can't reach. However, other storks often try to steal pieces of the nest, or even to take it over. Then the feathers fly!

People often help bird parents by building birdhouses or nesting boxes. No bird could build a birdhouse, so why do they lay their eggs in them? They think

◄ *At birth, a baby koala is barely three-quarters of an inch long. It stays in its mother's warm pouch for six months. Then the eight-inch baby koala is big enough to come out into the world.*

the birdhouse is a hollow tree. A hollow in a tree trunk is a safe place for a nest.

Some mammals build nests too. The nests provide shelter for babies who are still too young and weak to be out on their own. Foxes dig holes in the ground for their nests, called dens. Mice build nests out of many different things.

▼ *A mother fox does not pad her den. But her fur keeps her babies warm.*

▶ *This mouse has built a snug nest out of an old burlap sack.*

Their hairless, pink babies stay warm in the nest until they have grown fur and can find food on their own.

Of course, if an enemy does find a nest, the babies are no longer safe! The best thing would be for a nest to have legs. The mother wolf spider carries her nest

► *Koala mothers carry their babies piggyback style for about a year. Even when they are too big, koala babies try to crawl back into their mother's warm pouch.*

▼ *The wolf spider carries her nest, a cocoon, with her.*

on her back with her eggs or spiderlets inside. As long as she is safe her babies will be, too.

The mother koala is a traveling nest. First she carries her baby in her womb. After giving birth, she carries her tiny baby in a pouch on her belly. Next, the baby koala rides on her back, like a backpack. Opossums and kangaroos carry their babies in pouches too. Animals that do this are called marsupials.

▼ *This mother barn owl has found a safe corner high up in a barn to raise her babies.*

While some baby animals venture out on their own almost immediately, many must wait patiently for their parents to bring food back to the nest.

How often an animal has to go back and forth to feed its young depends on how much it can carry. An eagle's big talons hold a lot of food at once, but the starling makes a hundred trips or more each day to bring enough caterpillars and other bugs to feed its chicks.

▼ *This mother parakeet cares for her chicks in a nesting box.*

Owls, sparrows, and parakeets are nidicolous animals. This means the babies stay in the nest waiting to be fed by their parents. Chickens, ducks, and pheasants are able to see and walk right after hatching. Once the parent shows the chicks what to eat, the baby

birth. A half hour after it's born, a fawn stands on its wobbly legs. Soon it's running with the other deer.

People are truly nidicolous. They build fancy nests to shelter their helpless young. Sometimes these nests even have special rooms just for children!

birds can feed themselves. These independent birds are called nidifugous birds.

There are nidifugous and nidicolous mammals too. Herd animals like buffalo must be ready to move right after

▲ *Golden hamsters are nidicolous. The babies are dependent on their mother.*

▶ *The fawn is nidifugous. It must move along with the herd shortly after birth.*

A VISIT WITH MOTHER AND BABY

Animal mothers must take care of themselves. Many animal fathers simply fertilize the mother and then leave. Some other animal fathers even eat their own young!

But stickleback fish and sea horses are nurturing fathers. The male stickleback builds a nest where he cares for the female's eggs. Male sea horses keep the mother's eggs in a belly pouch like a marsupial. When the eggs hatch, it looks like the father is giving birth!

Many male birds bring food to the mother while she warms the eggs. Sometimes the male takes turns sitting on the nest. After the eggs are hatched, many bird parents also take turns feeding their young. Ducklings can feed themselves, but the father duck stays near his family to protect them from enemies.

Some insects, like bees, termites, and ants, live in huge groups called colonies. Each colony has one queen, who is the only egg layer. The queen lays so many eggs she has no time to take care of them. So every other insect in the colony helps the queen raise her young.

For instance, when an ant queen lays an egg, a worker ant carries it to a place in the anthill where it will be

◀ *This stork gathers grass for its nest.*

warm and dry. When the egg hatches, worker ants feed the larva. When the larva pupates, the workers carry the pupa to another special room where it finishes growing into an adult ant.

First the pupa chews a hole in its shell. Then a worker ant helps it emerge. The workers care for the young ant during the next few days while its body darkens and hardens. Then it is ready to work too!

A female cat is also called a queen. But she doesn't need workers to raise her kittens. In fact, most cats like to be left alone to birth and raise their kittens. You may prepare a basket or box for your pregnant cat, but she's more likely to have her kittens on the closet floor or under a bed.

If too many people come snooping around her nest, the mother cat will move her kittens. She carries them by

◄ *A pupa chews a hole in its shell.*
A worker ant helps enlarge the hole.
The tired young ant will spend the next few days resting while its armor hardens.

► *A mother cat carries her kitten to safety.*
The silent kitten hangs stiffly.

the back of the neck, but the kittens don't seem to mind. Mother hamsters do the same thing if they feel their babies are in danger.

Animal babies often get help coming into the world. Animals that live in

► *Dolphins help one another when a baby comes into the world.*

▼ *Hamsters also carry their young to safety.*

groups or herds help care for new mothers and their babies. Some lick the newborn baby or touch it tenderly. That way they get to know the baby as part of their herd.

Elephant cows protect a mother elephant while she's giving birth. Sometimes they help her tear open the amniotic sac. Sometimes they spray the new baby with sand to dry it off. Some elephant "aunts" even make extra milk for a new mother's baby.

Adult seagulls squabble with each other all the time. But they never hurt a baby seagull who is part of their flock. Grown-up monkeys defend any baby belonging to their troupe. Emperor penguins send their young to kindergarten! One adult cares for hundreds of baby penguins while the other adults hunt for food.

When a dolphin is born, several females called aunties hover around. The aunties keep other animals away. They also help the baby dolphin swim up to the surface for air. Then they watch as the young dolphin flips its tail and swims out to its first day of life.

Caring for babies of their own kind comes naturally for most animals. But sometimes there isn't enough food or space left for certain creatures because people or other animals have used it all up. Humans are realizing that some animal species won't survive without our help, and we're slowly learning to care for the babies of every species on earth. Perhaps you'll help too.